Breaking Bread

poems by

Catherine Marenghi

Finishing Line Press
Georgetown, Kentucky

Breaking Bread

Copyright © 2020 by Catherine Marenghi
ISBN 978-1-64662-114-9 First Edition
All rights reserved under International and Pan-American Copyright Conventions. No part of this book may be reproduced in any manner whatsoever without written permission from the publisher, except in the case of brief quotations embodied in critical articles and reviews.

ACKNOWLEDGMENTS

"The Elm Tree's Final Testament" was published in *Sisyphus*, Spring 2019.
"The Protest" won first-place honors from the Academy of American Poets University and College Poetry Prize program at Tufts University in 1976.
"Broken Bread" was published under the title "November" in the Summer 2018 issue of *Italian Americana*.
"Apple Blossoms" won first-place honors from the Academy of American Poets University and College Poetry Prize program at Tufts University in 1974.
"First Day of Kindergarten" was published in *Mobius: The Journal of Social Change* in the winter 2018 issue.
"Letter to My Son in Brooklyn" was selected by poet Jennifer Clement as first-place winner of the *Crossroads Magazine* poetry competition in 2019 and was published in the *Crossroads* 2019 annual edition.

Publisher: Leah Maines
Editor: Christen Kincaid
Cover Art: Todd James McIntosh
Author Photo: Todd James McIntosh
Cover Design: Elizabeth Maines McCleavy

Printed in the USA on acid-free paper.
Order online: www.finishinglinepress.com
also available on amazon.com

Author inquiries and mail orders:
Finishing Line Press
P. O. Box 1626
Georgetown, Kentucky 40324
U. S. A.

Table of Contents

The Elm Tree's Final Testament 1

My Father Had a Gun: A Pantoum 2

Wouldn't You Want 3

The Cardinal 5

The Protest 6

Cameo 8

Broken Bread 9

Apple Blossoms 10

The Young Poet as Fast-Food Waitress 11

Mother's Day 12

The Gift 13

What's Left 14

Restoration 15

Shredding Day 16

Grief 17

Things I Never Taught You 18

First Day of Kindergarten 19

A Letter to My Son in Brooklyn 21

To my son,
Steven Thomas Pfau

The Elm Tree's Final Testament

If I have my way, my death will come as a thunderclap,
    or the slap of a gruff wind that whips out of nowhere.
        In the snap of a twig, I'll be gone.

I who once feathered the summer shade of a quiet street,
    shook the rain from my leaves like a wet dog onto twirling
        umbrellas below, will not go quietly.

Uncharacteristically, I'll shout my parting words. I have stood
    in silence too long. I will groan and creek as I teeter,
        top-heavy after an ice storm, listing dangerously.

Wrinkled bark will buckle. Flailing branches will scratch at rooftops,
    snag and snap the power lines. My death will be greedy,
        clawing, snatching at anything I can take with me.

My root ball will rip up concrete sidewalks as I topple,
    nothing to break my fall, as I yank myself
        from the startled earth.

And when I am laid out flat and still, come close and see
    how I have lived. Now you can touch the fingertips
        of my furthest branches, tightly clenched buds

about to burst. Note the tender nests I nuzzled and warmed
    between my limbs. Hunger of beetles burrowing
        in my veins. All the life that I have loved.

Cut and split my broken limbs. Haul me away to be ground
    to mulch. And yet I will still be here. One sapling,
        lithe and strong, will give proof that I have lived.

My Father Had a Gun
A Pantoum

I've only ever held a gun
once: My father's hunting rifle.
It wasn't meant for sport, but for the kill
he skinned and boned for food.

Once my father's hunting rifle
bagged a deer, and a tender rabbit.
He skinned and boned them both for food.
He didn't have the coin to buy us meat.

He bagged a rabbit, even a tender squirrel,
to fill the empty plates around the table.
He didn't have the coin to buy us meat,
but there was always coin enough for beer.

To fill the seven plates around the table:
crooked carrots pulled from furrowed rows.
And there was always coin enough for beer,
but not for children's books or writing paper.

Crooked carrots pulled from furrowed rows
are not enough to feed a curious mind.
A child who asks for books and writing paper
cannot be sated by the hunt or harvest.

It's not enough to feed a hungry mind
with buckshot or with back-bending labor.
What cannot be sated by hunt or harvest
is much too quiet a thing to ever hold a gun.

Wouldn't You Want

If I close my eyes, I can hear it now: The car radio
softly plays, my brother at the wheel of the pink
and black '58 Rambler. We cruise the empty streets
at night. Summer of '71. Driving nowhere at all.

The lacquered streets unfurl before us. Radio dial
crackles with possibility. Dashboard lights smudge
our faces in regal hues, as the night splits itself open
for us to feast on its dark, glistening fruit.

All-night laundromats blaze with fluorescence
as we glide past. Neon Budweiser signs blink
from sleepy barrooms. Broken factory windows
grin with rows of twinkling teeth in our headlights.

The late-night DJ knows the songs we ache to hear,
impossible not to sing along. I carry the tune,
She's as sweet as Tupelo honey. My brother chimes in
low for the chorus: *She's an angel. She's an angel.*

Our own private concert on wheels, front-row seats.
All for us. *Nights in white satin, never reaching the end.*
For once we are the richest kids in town. Who
at this moment wouldn't give anything to be us?

Then guitar riffs announce the goddess—
Grace Slick is about to sing. My brother slows
to second gear, and we listen in hushed reverence:
When the truth is found to be-e-e-e-e lies...

And when the car makes its final turn—
the dead-end street, the ribbon of dirt driveway,
back to our splinter of a house at the edge
of town—we stay in the car till the final verse:

Don't you want somebody to love?
Don't you need somebody to love?
Wouldn't you love somebody to love?
You'd better find somebody to love.

The Cardinal

    My lover attacks the hardened
earth, pecking and pecking for seeds
under the flowering dogwood tree. Petals
fall like folded tongues.

    His brazen scarlet coat attracts human eyes
dangerously. They peer through slatted blinds,
sly and predatory. They do not see me blend
my soft brown plumes into drought-dusted leaves
and thirsty grass, my wingtips washed with just
a tinge of red, my beak ablaze.

    I hear my lover sing *who-it who-it*.
His supper song. But I don't leave my solid perch.
He comes to me. His beak is full, a string of
luscious seeds he gently rolls into my mouth,
kisses me beak to beak. I have my fill and then
he pulls away to dig for more.

    My lover needn't work so hard
to keep me. I am dizzy spinning my love for him,
circle of woven straw I wrap around and around
myself, love without end. I warm our clutch of
spotted eggs until they burst with strong beating
hearts, and gaping mouths that hunger,
as I hunger, too. His wet, earth-scented kiss.

The Protest

My father planted roses
to quiet himself,
to bury angry blood in the earth,
so it would rise and open
renewed, rich with the
ground's dark nutriment
in the heavy
black-veined blossoms.

And although the sacrament
repeated itself—
perennial petals drenched
and almost dripping with
the reddest wine—
he could not have enough.
He would take to his gardens again
and again. There were yellow roses,
hedge roses, seven sisters roses, each
of a different complexion, and
climbing ones mounted the pear tree.
Petals fell with the pears.

My father planted with such persistence,
trying to coax some grace from the earth,
while all around him—
> The organized corruption of
> brother and cousin, his own
> kind, even sacred womanhood,
> falling like dice on secret floors,
> shuffled and dealt like cards
> through a black hand—

With what bitterness he resigned to his gardens
to poultice his wounds with the healing earth,
to prod and torment the earth
into his own
unbridled protest
of roses.

Cameo

You never saw my mother in her nylon slip,
the kind with satin straps and lacy hem.

It's not what you think,
some delicate Madonna, finely
etched in carnelian shell,
oval locket of
gilded memory,
cast in a gilded frame.

No.
Hers was an image
to draw with a stick in sand,
hack out of stone,
broad-shouldered woman.

She never tilted her head
nor struck a pose.
Even Gauguin would have found her
too thick at the ankles and wrists.

But Gauguin never saw my mother
at the close of day,
stepping out of the rag she called
a dress, to emerge
dazzling
in her ivory gown.

Broken Bread

Forty-eight years it has already been:
November turned up its collar, chilled
at the sight of the children,
swarming a church to hear
a schoolmate's funeral mass.

For forty-eight years I have known about death,
and watched each autumn return
empty-handed,
the white winter holidays
brittle as bones.

There were times when I thought I could put it to words—
memorial poems, sweet retrospectives—

What made me think I could so organize sorrow
to take level cups of it, bake a great bread of it,
serve it with tea?

This death that bears
inexhaustible bounties,
thick with sharp stalks that sting,
shored away like seeds in a silo—
    It is not done.
    It is not done.

I would not wish
to break this bread
with anyone.

Apple Blossoms

Apple blossoms, torn from the bough,
transplanted in vases of cut
glass, are huddling expressions of
a fragrant life, a re-
interpretation of life, where air
unfolds into layers of air,
whiteness breaks
into multiples of petals,
edged in pink, curled,
clustering over and over again,
articulating self upon delicate self.

So we see them.
So we align our senses into
compositions, designating
apple blossoms
to mean
something apart from orchards
and from trees,
translating them into the
pure sense we have of their
fragility, immaculate beauty,
longings of ours
artfully arranged.

And yet the other sense
of apple blossoms remains,
their own
reason for being
remains,
resists interpretation:

Like a remembrance, tucked
in the folds of their petals,
the unmistakable scent
of fresh apples.

The Young Poet as Fast-Food Waitress

For the one behind the counter,
she who waits on the hungry
faces and hands,
whose collar is brown
with the sweat of her neck, whose shoes
are lined with aches, for her
there are no green, grass-scented poems
to write, no ferns and mosses
wet from a rain, to quench
an impulse to praise.

But if there is acknowledgment,
this can suffice:

To hear with her full ear
        the grills spitting grease,
        the tip jar guzzling metal coins,
        the toddler's wail after spilling
        his icy orange drink on his knees,
not as a deadening blur, to be gotten over
and done with, but
specifics, facts,
things to be known and felt as true.

To know, and therefore to write,
that all the crumbs and drippings
and discarded wrappings
are real,
and as audible as the rain,
and as clear as the distant sky.

Mother's Day

May 14 at downtown crossing.
Macy's banner gushes, *Give*
the gift of beauty for Mother's Day.
Perfumes hang thick
in the air, unrecognizable
as candied fruits.

My mother wore a different scent
when she walked up
from the fields in the morning.
Fingernails black
with fresh dirt.
Bits of leaf and moss
clung to her calloused
feet.

She smelled
like a garden.

The Gift

We gave you this death,
Celia, after the doctors said
your brain's gentle humming traffic
ceased.

We gave you this death, Celia.
Why don't you open it?
Cut the ribbons, see
how it cuts you free.

Un-fasten your life, pluck
the I-Vs out like hairpins, pull
the tape, the gauze, unravel yourself,
let your life fall
like hair running down your back.

Can you see yourself? As your spirit
rises up from your johnny,
can you see how smooth and still
your body lies,
like a freshly made bed?

Do you see our mother
drawing back the sheets to touch
your feet, your hands, the way
a new mother checks
her baby's fingers and toes?

And now, as the nurses come to collect you
(through watered eyes they seem
a fluttering of pale blue angels)—
do you see them chariot you away?

Does it comfort you, my sister,
now that we gave you this death?

What's Left

Every time I visit, I am born anew to her.
Turning her wheeled chair to face the sun,
I bend down to remind her—*I am your daughter.*
She studies my face, says I'm strangely pretty—
not recognizing, yet seeing what only
a mother's eyes could see.

Her dinner, an unrecognizable trio
of beige purees, sits untouched on her tray.
She, a once-sturdy farm girl, able
to swing an ax or push a plow with a man's
strength, now can't lift a spoon to her mouth,
or know what for.

Her son and grandson enter the room
like solemn butlers, bearing pies in outstretched
hands: her favorites, pumpkin and mincemeat.
We tell her it is Christmas Day, as if the words
will coax her standoffish memory—
shake loose the distant days of
fragrant roasts in speckled pans,
wood-fired ovens, warm milk in pails
fresh from the barn, Great Depression years
she'd say were lean but never wanting.

We circle round her like a Christmas tree,
knowing she's been lopped off
from the roots of her memory.

We keep our hopes prickly and green
long past their time.

Restoration

Whenever I see an old abandoned house, the mother in me
wants to cradle it, kiss its wounds and make it better.
This one's a Queen Anne revival, cryptic whim of a house
with wings and bays, turrets like rockets aimed for the moon.

Rooms with names they don't use any more, like sitting room,
dressing room, boudoir. Nurseries once a rumpus of toddlers
in lace collars and button-up boots. Chandeliers that swayed
to the waltz of ball-gown gatherings, windows blinking with
molten candlelight.

Now the only sound is the chain saws gashing the towering trees,
chipping the overgrown rhododendrons, making way
for the wrecking ball. They'll level the place, the bastards.

Then they'll throw up one of those vinyl-clad monstrosities
with central air, three-car garage, and open floor plan.
An oversized bully, taking over this quarter-acre lot, and
probably only one or two people will live there.

I want to stand this ground in protest. Block the bulldozers with
my body, lay down on the parquet floors, rescue the mantels and
dentil moldings, save the mullioned windows and fish-scale shingles.

But then, how many picket signs can one person carry?
The world is architected with too much need.

Shredding Day

When it comes to the final tally, all
the daily transactions, canceled checks,
tax returns, spiraling audit trails
enough to circle
earth and moon.

So much attention paid,
so many years spent, on filling
file folders, thick with memos,
statements, lists, demands for payment.
So much rectitude
of the highest moral
order, bathed in ink and fury,
thousands of paper scraps with my
signature, my guarantee,
my promise.

Mechanical teeth pull and grind
forty years of rectitude
destined for the recycling bin—
one more act
of rectitude. Where
does it end, if not in the lions' manes
of pulp and paper,
teeth gnashing and gnawing toward
the final double-entry ledger
marking the profit and loss,
the deficit
of days.

Grief

Tahlequah, the orca mother,
keeps her dead calf afloat,
nudges it through Puget Sound
a thousand miles, seventeen days.
She forms a tight coven with six
other orcas, drawing a circle
around their grief, tracing
a moonbeam's footprint under the night.

The elephant matriarch, Victoria,
rests along the banks of the
Ewaso Nyiro, never to rise again.
Her daughter stays behind after
the herd moves on, ramming
her mother's body with her head until
she understands, and later
returns to caress the gentle bones.

My mother's feral cat, Sammy,
black-spotted pan handler, begs daily
for food. She birthed her young
in the lupine patch, but wild dogs
came for them. She still stops
at the weedy undergrowth,
staring at their absence.

Tahlequah. Victoria, Sammy.

All animals grieve.
Don't we?

Things I Never Taught You

You found a dead mouse inside the dank garage.
Just four years old, you recognized the face of death.
Running late for work, I thought I'd toss the creature
in the trash, when you said, *No. We have to bury it.*

And so we chose the soft mulch beside the lilac trees,
and used a tattered rag to shroud the poor thing.
With garden trowel I scraped a shallow grave, and just
as I had laid the tiny corpse to rest, you said, *Wait.
It needs a name. We can't bury it without a name!*

And in that moment, I could see the strong insistent
roots of something I had never planted. Instincts that
were finer than my own. You were not an empty vessel
into which I'd pour my stored wisdom.

In acts of love, you would be my teacher.

First Day of Kindergarten

I can't wait to meet my son's first
teacher. I'm bursting to tell her
all about my brilliant child.
Just last night, his eyes fixed
on an unobstructed moon, he said:

> *Lightning makes a lot of noise.*
> *And thunder makes a lot of noise.*
> *But the moon is very quiet.*

I scrambled to write it down, one more
for the keepsake book, and my maternal
thoughts careen off to a starry future,
where my son writes a shimmering poetry
book entitled
The Moon Is Very Quiet.

I can't wait to tell the teacher
about this budding poet, tell her
he reads me the headlines
from *The New York Times,*
not to brag, but she needs to know
my son can read. He has his own
library card, and carries home stacks
of books that spill like joy from
his little arms.

And he can spin stories
that magically mash together
Snow White, the Power Rangers,
Brunhild from Wagner's Ring Cycle,
Robert DeNiro, and Martha Stewart.
His imagination is a sprawling house
that welcomes all comers.

And he can spell, even the really
tricky words, like *neighbor*, and *elephant*.
His mind is a camera that takes
mental pictures of words.

So I begin by asking his teacher
what books they'll read in school that year.

She looks at me with blank eyes,
and tells me her focus will be
on developing fine motor skills.

And now I'm having second thoughts
about leaving my gifted son with her,
fearing she will prune and trim
his wild and blossoming mind.

I drive away and wonder—why
fine motor skills, and not
rainbow fish and secret gardens,
bulls named Ferdinand,
or even the alphabet song?

I switch on my headlights at 9
in the morning, just to lift me from
my deepening gloom.

And all I can think of
is the day when I'll get the call
to tell me a man in a black trench coat
has opened fire on the tiny
chairs and desks,
and I wonder if my son will be the one
who crawls out from under his teacher's
body, finds the phone in her purse and taps
nine - one - one
using his fine motor skills.

A Letter to My Son in Brooklyn

You were 14 when I asked.
We both already knew the answer.

I will always love you, is what I said.
What I meant was *I am so afraid.*
Someone will hate you, tie you to a post
in the name of some unspeakable god.
Someone will lay hands on that perfect body,
long and slight as you are, a pea tendril.
And it won't be in the name of love.

You were 16. Your stomach pain
turned out to be a collapsed lung.
You lay back in your hospital bed,
and opened your johnny, revealing
a still-hairless chest, smooth as poured
milk. The doctor smeared it with
something orange, and sliced into your
skin with a scalpel, as if that were a
normal thing to do in a mother's presence.
I couldn't let you see my face. I slipped
into the hall and crumpled to the floor.

The truth is, I've never been strong.
I never could protect you, not from scalpels,
words, or other pointed things.

You're 27. Soon you'll load a U-Haul truck
and drive from Brooklyn to Idaho
with a man as tall and slender as you.
The one you talked to all night long
in the Chinese restaurant. You'll cross
a dozen states where they permit
open carry
of hatred.

Would it make any difference if I said—
My darling boy—Be careful.

Catherine Marenghi is an award-winning poet and memoirist. Her poems have been published in literary journals and anthologies in the U.S. and Mexico. A native of Massachusetts, she writes with a profound sense of place and keen insights into family bonds, love, loss, and the longing for home.

The acclaimed poet Richard Blanco selected her poem "Long-Awaited Man" as first-place winner in a 2018 poetry competition sponsored by *Crossroads Magazine*. Commenting on her poem, Blanco described "a deft command of figurative language and metaphor, which are the essence of poetry. ... Catherine Marenghi unravels and elucidates the complexities of longing, passion and love."

Poet Jennifer Clement selected her poem "Letter to My Son in Brooklyn" as first-place winner in the same *Crossroads* competition in 2019. Clement said, "The poem is original and both fierce and tender, which gives an uncommon tension."

Her poems, including "The Protest," have twice won first-place honors from the Academy of American Poets University and College Poetry Prize program at Tufts University. Her poem "The Affair" won first-place honors at the Marblehead Festival of the Arts in Marblehead, MA. Most recently her work has appeared in *Sisyphus, Crossroads, Solamente en San Miguel, Italian Americana, Mobius: Journal of Social Change, Phi Kappa Phi Forum, Conclave,* and *Peregrine Journal*.

Catherine's published writings include the 2016 memoir *Glad Farm* a powerful story of poverty, resilience, and the triumph of life over death. The book describes her childhood in a one-room farmhouse on a former gladiolus farm, and it has been compared with *The Glass Castle*. Among its many endorsements, former President Jimmy Carter called it "inspiring."

Catherine also has ghost-authored two nonfiction works. She holds an M.A., B.A. Summa Cum Laude in English from Tufts University, where she studied with poets Denise Levertov and X. J. Kennedy.

The parent of an adult son, Catherine recently retired early from a career spanning journalism, business writing, and entrepreneurship, and currently divides her time between San Miguel de Allende, Mexico, and Wareham, Massachusetts.

www.ingramcontent.com/pod-product-compliance
Lightning Source LLC
LaVergne TN
LVHW041519070426
835507LV00012B/1673